Want to get started investing in the stock market, but aren't sure how to do so?

What are stocks?

What determines their market prices?

Why do they go up and down?

How can you beat the stock market?

What are mutual funds?

What are index funds?

What are Exchanged Traded Funds?

Even though the stock market is the heart of a country's wealth, and even though it enables everybody to be a part owner in the largest, most successful countries in the world, it's not taught in public schools.

But be warned: the mainstream press often misrepresents the stock market. They focus on making the news exciting and dramatic to sell copies.

Frankly, the best investing is boring investing. It's putting as much money as you can afford into many companies, and reinvesting dividends. And continuing to do so until you retire.

The best investing is not about trying to figure out what's going to happen in the economy or the markets tomorrow, next week, next month or next year.

Many financial writers try to make you think you have to work hard at investing. You must study stock charts every night. Read annual reports. Thoroughly analyze a company's financial statements. Read THE WALL STREET JOURNAL, BARRON'S, and MONEY MAGAZINE. Buy special software. Hang out in online investing forums.

Not so!

Don't waste your time. This book takes modern financial

theory to its logical conclusion. You can get the maximum long term benefit by following its simple plan. No tedious math or economics theory needed.

It's simple to set up. Then you forget about it. Pay no attention to the financial news. Just focus on making the most money you can in your career or business, that's all.

And if you're starting small, we've got you covered to.

You'll learn the various kinds of stocks and the various ways to invest in them, including tax-deferred retirement accounts such as an IRA.

Warning: the investment world is full of people who think your money should belong to them.

From out and out scammers, brokers, financial advisors, newsletter editors, and to the managers of actively traded mutual funds, if you're not careful you'll help everybody get rich except yourself.

Stock Market Investing for Beginners

How Anyone Can Have a Wealthy Retirement by Ignoring Much of the Standard Advice and Without Wasting Time or Getting Scammed

Richard Stooker

ISBN-13: 978-1466464988

ISBN-10: 1466464984

Copyright © 2012 by Richard Stooker and Gold Egg Investing LLC

Cover graphic design by Drew of idrewdesign

Book cover and graphic design Copyright © 2012 by Richard Stooker and Gold Egg Investing, LLC

DISCLAIMER

I am not a broker.

I am not a licensed securities dealer or representative of any kind.

I am no legal right to sell you securities and I'm not trying to do so.

Nothing in this book is to be construed as a solicitation or offer to sell you securities.

Nothing in this book is to be construed as personal financial advice.

I have no legal right to give you personal financial advice. Even if I were a registered financial advisor, I don't know you or your individual financial situation.

This book is the result of my research and is believed accurate. It consists of my opinions and suggestions.

I'm not making any representations as to how much money you will make if you invest according to the guidelines I set forth—that will depend upon the payouts of dividends and interest of the precise securities you decide to invest in, and nobody can predict the future.

That is part of the problem with mainstream financial advice—it assumes the future will repeat the past. It doesn't.

Past performance is not indicative of future results.

This book is for education and entertainment.

Nothing in this book is to be construed as professional advice. For that, you should consult your attorney, accountant or financial adviser.

I am not responsible for the results of your investment decisions.

I follow my own advice. The only financial investments I own, besides ordinary checking, savings and money market accounts, in my IRAs and my taxable brokerage account, are ones I recommend in this book.

I am not seeking to raise the price of those securities by making them more popular. I will not sell them unless driven by financial emergency.

You must read, think over what I say, make your own investment decisions and take responsibility for your own life, including the results of your investment decisions.

Continuing to read this book implies your acceptance of these terms.

LEGAL NOTICE

Table of Contents

Introduction

My goals:

1. Get you started in the stock market and headed toward to a wealthy retirement

2. Show you how to avoid wasting time and money

3. Keep it short and easy to read

I know a lot of people are ignorant about how the stock market can benefit them. I see the questions they ask on Yahoo Answers, LinkedIn and in the comments section of a video I posted on YouTube explaining the stock market.

There's a lot of misinformation being spread about the stock market. A lot of it comes from the major media outlets and writers. A lot of websites and bloggers spread confusion along with good insights.

Plus, a lot of people seem to think all there is to succeeding in the stock market is to learn THE technique or the formula, and all they need to do is ask and someone will tell them.
My aim is to give you the knowledge not just to buy a few shares of stock, but to start building a personal fortune without making the many mistakes I have.

I will warn you—some of my opinions are NOT mainstream investing advice.

For example: many financial writers want you to believe it takes a lot of time, money, and effort to invest in stocks.

Not true.

There is a key fact about stock market investing (commonly accepted by financial academics, and such industry giants as John Bogle who founded Vanguard) that I alone (that I know of) take to its logical extreme.

That's good news because it means you don't have to learn a bunch of formulas, how to analyze company books, how to read charts, hang on in investing forums online, buy trading software or anything else like that.

Heck, you don't even have to read The Wall Street Journal.

That's all a waste of your time.

I spent nearly 20 years trying to get rich quick. I read countless books on how to choose winning stocks. I went to seminars. I bought programs.

I once bought a stock one day and saw it go up 60% the next day. Nice one, but why? I didn't know, so it wasn't useful. I once tried to get rich with covered calls. They're considered extremely "conservative," but the stock I bought sank so low I still lost money. I once put on a United States Treasuries bond option trade with a 90% success rate. Thanks to a meltdown by the Russian Stock Exchange, I lost all my money.

My B.S. Accounting degree helped me understand the basics of what I was doing, it was no help when it came to actually making money.

Then one day my mother asked me to organize her financial records. She showed me the notebook containing a list of the stocks my grandfather bought for her with the insurance money she received from my father's premature death in an automobile accident.

That happened in 1955, yet my mother still had that notebook. She never threw anything away :)

Looking at it, I realized my grandfather had chosen a well-rounded portfolio of stocks that paid dividends.

Many of them had been sold over the years, or bought up, but others were still sending my mother substantial quarterly dividend checks: Hershey, Wrigley, AT&T and its descendants, Ralston Purina, and others.

Those investments enabled my mother to raise two small children—myself and my sister. And after we grew up and began supporting ourselves, it allowed her to live well in comfort.

And it struck me—dividends were the key.

So I'm telling you upfront investing for income is my prejudice.

However, I'm not forcing you to believe me—and since you're a beginner, at this point you may not have a strong opinion, but just be wondering, because doesn't everybody else in the world just "assume" that "investing" in the stock market means buying some stock and then selling it—hopefully for a profit?

Yes, that's what most people think, without ever examining it.

Heck, you may not even know what dividends are. The modern mainstream financial press pretty much ignores them or treats them as unimportant.

And if I don't convert you to investing for income, that's all right.

I know the optimal way to investing for higher stock prices, and I'll explain that to you too.

The best part is, investing the way I advise is easy and simple.

A lot of people make it sound hard and complicated. They want you to study graphs, read company annual reports, and run countless spreadsheets to analyze company numbers—or spend hours a day online talking to other people who do the same thing.

There's no evidence any of that is useful.

In fact, there's tons of evidence—research studies going back decades—it doesn't work.

I'll tell you the REAL "secret" to making more money, and how you should therefore spend your extra time to make more money from investing.

Let's start at the beginning—

What is stock?

Chapter 1

What is Stock?

A share of stock is a unit of ownership in a corporation.

This may seem a little odd or too simple, but at root that's all it is.

Example:

As of February 2011, Microsoft had about 8.4 billion shares outstanding.

Bill Gates owns about 591 million shares, making him a 7% owner.

He is the largest single owner. Other important Microsoft executives also own big chunks. The rest is owned by the general public—that's you and me.

If you buy 100 shares of Microsoft stock, you are a 100/8,400,000,000th (or 1/84,000,000th) owner of one of the largest companies on Earth.

You're not going to catch up with Gates, at least not with Microsoft stock :)

(Starting your own successful company is the way to get superwealthy from the stock market, but is not the subject of this book.)

You may not feel like much of an "owner" of the company because you have no practical control over what Microsoft does (you don't even qualify for a discount on Microsoft Office), but legally that's exactly what you are, and it has some potentially important legal and financial implications for you.

This Book is About Common Stock

Shares of stock ownership in a company are known as "common" stock, and that's the subject of this book.

There is such a thing as "preferred" stock, but it's different, and not the subject of this book.

Whenever you hear people bragging about selling stock for a profit, or the New York Stock Exchange, or their stockbroker, or the Dow Jones Industrial Average, they're referring to common stock.

Common Stock Ownership Means:

1. You become a part owner in the company, in proportion to how many shares you own.

2. If the company's Board of Directors declares a payment of dividends, you will receive the same per-share payment as every other common stock owner.

3. You have the right to attend annual stockholder meetings and to vote on proposed changes and on who is on the board of directors.

You get one vote per share of stock you own.

So you do have a say-so in how Microsoft is run, but at 100 shares it's a lot smaller than Bill Gates'.

4. If the company goes out of business, you have the right to receive whatever is left over after its legal debts and the lawyers are paid, in

proportion to how many shares you own.

So, in summary a share of common stock is a unit of ownership in a corporation.

But what are corporations?

Chapter 2

What are Corporations?

A corporation is company recognized by the government as an entity separate from any persons.

Its existence can continue indefinitely.

It can carry on business. Assuming it makes profit, it owes taxes and must pay them.

Why Have Corporations:

1. Because the corporation is a separate entity, it can continue doing business despite all changes in people.

Coca-Cola didn't die with Asa Candler. McDonalds didn't die with Ray Kroc. And Disney didn't die with Walt.

2. They can raise money from investors who get to share in the profits without doing any work.

Most companies are started by one or a group of people who are not (yet) fabulously wealthy. They need more money to expand their company, so they sell a part of its ownership to the stock market.

3. Limited liability

This is very important. Nobody would buy shares of stock if they thought they could be personally sued for what the corporation does.

There are thousands of companies listed on American stock exchanges. They are engaged in many kinds of businesses. They are legally obligated to make as much money as possible.

Sometimes they bend the rules. Sometimes they break the law.

Sometimes they think they're obeying the law, but the government thinks otherwise.

The vast majority do the best they can to keep employees and customers safe and happy, but accidents happen.

And lawyers need to support their families.

So, sometimes rightly and sometimes wrongly, companies get sued.

Sometimes they win in court and sometimes they lose.

No matter how much money a company is ordered to pay, nobody will ever ask you—although you're one of the owners—to pay anything out of your pocket.

To the extent the company loses cash because of a lawsuit, you the owner of 100 shares are disadvantaged, but nobody can ever ask you to pay extra.

In contrast, think about what would happen if you owned a store, and somebody slipped and died from hitting their head on the floor and you didn't have insurance.

Do you think that person's family would sue you for every dime you own?

You better believe it.

And if you had any partners, the family's lawyers would also sue them even if they had nothing to do with the store's floor.

When you own stock, the worst that can happen is the company goes out of business and you lose the entire amount you paid for the stock.

That's not a happy situation, but it beats losing your home and retirement savings because a minimum wage employee forgot to put out a "Wet Floor" sign when they mopped a floor.

One of the signs carried by Occupy Wall Street protestors is:

"Corporations are Not People."

True.

Corporations are Collections of People

It should be obvious, but while corporations are NOT people, they ARE made up of people.

Corporations have employees. From the janitor to the Chief Executive Officer (CEO), they all work for the corporation. It's easy for upper management (which has most of the power) to forget the corporation is an entity separate from them, but it's legally true.

Corporations also have owners. Everybody who owns at least one share of stock is a part owner of the corporation.

Corporations also have a Board of Directors which is supposed to represent the interests of shareholders, and therefore make sure management is doing its job.

Upper management and the Board of Directors are supposed to run the corporation so it makes as much money as possible. This is a legal obligation they have to the shareholders.

(Remember, the CEO—although the big boss in charge of everything—is technically just the hired help, while stockholders are the owners. But most CEOs also own a lot of shares of stock.)

Of course, because everybody concerned is a human being, there can be—and often are—differences in opinion as to what is best for the corporation.

It's easy for investors and stock market analysts and commentators to forget this but, because they're made up of people, over time corporations do change.

If you're young you may find this difficult to believe, but in the 1960s and 1970s IBM was the most respected corporation in the United States. Unless you're a techie, may you not have even heard of IBM.

Some companies are old. Coca-Cola started around 1919. Obviously, the people who launched it are all gone. It's the "same" corporation on paper. It still owns the secret formula. It still sells soft drinks. But in many ways it's changed a lot. And it's had its ups and downs.

No matter how hard companies try to pass along the "old ways" of doing things, sooner or later the older generation retires and new people move up, bringing new ways of doing things which may be better—or worse—or some of both.

So corporations are separate entities owned by people who have the right to buy and sell the corporation's stock.

Which happens through a stock exchange.

Chapter 3

What is a Stock Exchange

A stock exchange is simply where the buying and selling of shares of stock is organized.

Back in 1693 England's stockbrokers hung out in coffee houses along Exchange Alley. By 1698 a broker named John Castaing was regularly posting lists of stock prices in Jonathan's Coffee House. That was the beginning of the London Stock Exchange.

A hundred years later, on May 17, 1792, 24 stockbrokers signed an agreement under a buttonwood tree outside 68 Wall Street in lower Manhattan. That was the beginning of the New York Stock Exchange.

On the floor of the exchange, traders buy and sell shares of stocks based on the orders they receive from stockbrokers.

It's in the format of a continuous auction.

Buyers negotiate with sellers to reach a price they can both accept.

Let's say you tell your broker to buy you a "round lot" (100 shares) of Microsoft. (Any number of shares less than 100 is an "odd lot.")

Because that's a small amount, your order is grouped with other customers, and they send an order to a representative on the floor of the

New York Stock Exchange.

Through what looks like confused shouting, that person finds someone who is selling Microsoft. They negotiate on the price.

If that seems rather quaint, inefficient and…old-fashioned (not to mention 20th century) you're right.

In 1971 the National Association of Securities Dealers started the NASDAQ computerized exchange, though at that time it was basically a computer bulletin board. Now NASDAQ is the second largest stock exchange in the world (behind the New York Stock Exchange), and it's still all-electronic.

Eventually the New York Stock Exchange will be all electronic as well, but nobody knows when.

For us, it doesn't matter. Both systems work.

The New York Stock Exchange is now owned by Euronext, a company formed from four European stock exchanges merging, so you may see it referred to as Euronex: New York. But for now, for most people in the US, it's still the New York Stock Exchange.

Most countries of the world now have at least one stock exchange. It's a sign of being modern.

Many beginners have the ambition to beat the stock market. Or think they have to beat it to make money from stocks. Let's think about what exactly that means.

Chapter 4

What Does It Mean to Beat the Stock Market?

This book does not promise to teach you how to beat the market for many reasons which will be clearer by the time you finish.

However, it is a concern of many investors. And many new investors ask how they can do it.

What does that even mean?

Officially, to beat the market you must have a portfolio of stock shares which rise in price more than the market as a whole, on a risk-adjusted basis, and in the long run.

That "risk-adjusted basis" is an important qualification.

There are stocks which can be "high flyers." Given a good market, they'll go up a lot more than the market.

Yet in a bad market, they often fall even lower than the market.

Heck, you can take all your money to a casino, find a roulette table and bet it all on one number.

Sure you'll probably lose it all. But if 100 people do it, two to four will win and get paid $35 for every dollar they bet.

100 people do the same thing. Several of them win big while everybody else loses. Can we say the winners "beat" the roulette wheel—or just were the lucky ones?

That's the nature of risk. You can win big, but you'll more likely lose.

And beating the market for real means doing it in the long run.

In any given year roughly half the money managers in the world will beat the market. Most of them will underperform the market next year.

Flipping a coin and getting heads two or three times in a row does not make you a skillful coin flipper.

Fortunately, it's not necessary to beat the market.

It is necessary for you to be clear on what's called your investment horizon or timeline.

Chapter 5

What is Your Investing Horizon?

A lot of investing books and financial advisors make a big deal out of what's called your investing "horizon."

That comes down to, how long to you plan to keep your money invested?

In some ways it's an important question, but in another way it isn't.

Some people's "horizon" is ten minutes—certainly under one day.

Those are day traders. All their trades are short-term. They close out all their stock positions when they shut down for the day.

Other people are speculators who hope to make a profit from a stock within a week or several months.

Others are willing to hold stocks for a few years before they sell for a profit.

True "investors" are building wealth for the long-term, to fund their retirements or to leave their families a large estate. They are looking ahead twenty, thirty, fifty or even more years.

This can make a big difference.

A stock of a promising company can appear to have a great future for the next several years—but be going downhill today because of some bad news about a product launch.

The day trader is selling while the several years speculator is buying.

Sometimes you will hear people talk or write about how there are two sides to every trade, and only one is right.

But this really isn't true. The day trader selling a stock they see going downhill today may be just as glad to get out before it goes down further as the several years speculator is glad to pick up the stock at a low price today so they can sell it at a higher profit (they believe) in two years.

Both buyer and seller can be happy, and meet their trading goals, if they have different horizons.

So what is your investing horizon?

That depends on your investment goals.

Chapter 6

What are Your Investment Goals?

Are you learning about stock investing to save up money to pay for a house?

Go on an expensive vacation?

Put a child (who's already out of the third grade) through college?

Have an emergency fund in case of a lay off, illness or other family disaster?

If so, I have just one thing to say to you—

Don't.

The stock market is much too volatile and unpredictable to use it to fund anything within the next ten years, and preferably more.

(That's why I qualified the "child" as being out of the third grade. If your child is still ten or more years away from college, you may consider putting those funds into stocks.)

It's be a shame for you to work and scrimp and save and be just about to pay for that round the world cruise, and then see half your savings wiped out in a fast crash. It could happen.

Many financial experts claim stocks have always made money in any given 20 year period during the 20th century. I don't believe that's totally true—after the 1929 crash it took stocks over 25 years (from August 1929 to November 1954) to regain the ground they lost.

But it is true for most 20 year periods. But in some of those 20 year periods—the ones ending in bear markets—it's BARELY true. Stocks made money, but only a little.

And you're not planning to take 20 years to save up a house downpayment or for a vacation.

And to put your emergency fund in the stock market is downright foolish.

As I write these words in October 2011, the Dow is at 11,577.

The mainstream media would have you cheering because it's up a lot since the March 2009 bear market bottom.

But it first reached 11,500 in very late 1999.

Therefore, the stock market has gone exactly nowhere for the past dozen years.

Yes, you may remind me, it went up to over 14,000 in October 2007, but that's past and gone. Over. Finished.

Nobody knows when it will reach 14,000 again.

And not too long ago, the market was around 10,700, which it first reached in 1998.

If you had put a lumpsum of cash into the market in 1998 when it was first at 10,700 and sold the stocks in September 2011, you'd just about have broken even.

The stock market can make you fabulously wealthy, but NOT overnight.

It's for long term wealth, and "long term" is not one year. It's 20 or more.

Besides, there is a way to get wealthy from the stock market even when it does not go up in price. We'll get to that in a later chapter.

The lesson for this chapter is stock investing is for the long haul—retirement or very distant expenses (such as college while your child is still learning to read).

Short term money belongs in a money market account, savings account or certificates of deposit.

When you realize the stock market is only for long term money, you keep your short term money in a safe place, and you are miraculously free from worrying about the stock market in the short term.

But almost everybody else does, which is a mistake.

Chapter 7

The Next 30 Years

If you pay any attention to the mainstream financial media and most commentators and analysts, you can see they all have a bad case of nearsightedness.

I've worn thick glasses since I was a kid, so I know what I'm talking about.

"Stocks went down today because unemployment remains high."

"Stocks went up today on news European leaders are close to an agreement on how to prevent a Greek bankruptcy."

"X's price went up today because sales of its new product were unexpectedly strong."

"Y's price went down today because the US dollar rose against the Japanese yen, so sales volume in Asia may go down."

"Z's price went up today because first quarter earnings per share were one cent higher than expected."

"Z's price went down today because second quarterly earnings per share were one cent lower than expected."

All they look at is the prospects for today and the near future.

Mutual fund managers have to do this, because they're evaluated by their quarterly bottom lines.

That gives you a big advantage over them. You can see farther. You can choose stocks for the long term future.

Coca-Cola had its IPO in 1919. Do you think that company has had some downs as well as ups in the past 92 years? Of course. Several decades ago some company executives made a major blunder. They took the traditional cola soda off the market and replaced it with "New Coke"— which everybody hated.

It's one of the biggest marketing blunders a modern corporation has ever committed.

I can't tell you how many quarters KO "disappointed" analysts by falling short of earnings expectations and estimates, but I'm sure over the years it's had its share of such quarters.

Should you have sold then? But if your grandparents had bought one share for $40 at the IPO price, and reinvested all your dividends, and left that portfolio to you, it'd now be worth over $5 million dollars.

Would you care about New Coke and quarterly disappointments nobody now remembers or cares about?

Obviously not.

All right, you're not now concerned with making your grandchildren wealthy.

Just put on your 30-year glasses for a moment.

I know that sounds like a looooooooonnnnnnggggggg time, especially if you're young.

But the younger you are, the more likely you are to survive that entire time, and many years afterward.

Trust me—the years will go by faster than you realize.

If you're under 65, you should plan your finances on the assumption you're going to live at least another 30 years, because you most likely are.

Now, in case it's not obvious, I don't know the details of the future, but we can see some obvious things:

1. Political changes—some good, some bad

2. Local wars, revolutions, disasters and catastrophes

3. Technological advances

4. Barring a humongous, large-scale catastrophe, the world as a whole will continue to get wealthier, just as it's been doing for decades, despite #1 and #2.

One thing you must remember is it's very unlikely—barring a huge worldwide catastrophe—the world is going to abandon capitalism as the basic economic system.

That means the world thirty years from now is going to have stock exchanges and stocks. And money will be just as important as it is now.

Therefore, a diverse portfolio of high quality stocks is going to be worth a lot more then than now—even though that portfolio will have many ups and downs (including DEEP downs)—between now and then.

If you take my advice and buy only stocks that pay dividends—and reinvest the dividends—that portfolio could make you wealthy beyond your current dreams.

But even if you invest for capital gains, you're going to be far ahead.

Now, it's true I can't give you a guaranteed promise of this.

The companies you buy today are going to change. Some will change their names, some will be bought out. Some will go out of business.

That's why you shouldn't depend on any one or two stocks, but invest in an index, so you benefit from the economic advances of the world.

It's true I can't 100% guarantee that, but what can stop it?

The world has grown and advanced in both wealth and freedom for hundreds of years, despite wars, economic depressions, revolutions, dictatorships, and natural disasters. It will continue to do so unless there's an extremely large disaster.

For example:

1. Worldwide ecological catastrophe

2. Worldwide nuclear war

3. Worldwide bio-chemical warfare

4. A large comet or asteroid strikes the Earth

5. We're invaded by hostile aliens

6. The sun goes nova

7. Communism takes over the world, and stock exchanges are all torn down.

Now notice something about those (remote) science fictional possibilities:

if one were to happen, you'd either be dead or struggling to survive, or forbidden to invest.

The loss of your stock portfolio would be the least of your problems.

I've read a lot of doomsday novels (I'm a science fiction fan), and I can't remember any scene where a character gets upset about losing their stock portfolio. Picture Road Warrior Mad Max crying in the desert because he didn't have time to sell off his stocks before civilization was destroyed. It's ludicrous.

So the future 30+ years out comes down to two general scenarios

1. Worldwide catastrophe

In which case you won't care about stocks anyway.

2. Greater wealth and prosperity for humanity as a whole—though we'll still have pockets of poverty and many other problems.

(I'm not predicting Utopia in 30 years.)

If the future is #2, you'll be breaking your arm patting yourself on the back for having the smarts to buy stock back in 2012 when it was so cheap.

So, ignore ALL short-term market thinking and speculating.

Buy good stocks. Hold. Reinvest dividends.

Never sell unless:

1. You have a financial emergency

2. The company is on the brink of going out of business

Ignore the short term financial news. You'll sleep a lot more soundly and your portfolio will be a lot safer.

Chapter 8

What is Compounding

Compounding earnings refers to how your money grows when it makes money, and that money is then used to generate more money.

It's like the old "brain teaser" I read as a kid.

A boy tells his father that if Dad'll give the boy money every day for a month, beginning with a penny on Day 1, he'll never ask his father for money again.

But the catch is, every day the father must give the boy double what he gave the day before.

Day 1 was 1 cent.

Day 2 was 2 cents.

Day 3 was 4 cents.

Day 4 was 8 cents.

This is a harmless game, the father thinks.

By Day 30, it's $5,368,709.12.

Unfortunately, I don't know of any legitimate investments that can double every day. However, the basic principle remains.

It's also worth noting money you don't invest—or lose to unnecessary expenses—also compounds in a negative fashion, by its ABSENCE.

Therefore, minimizing expenses is an important, underappreciated way to increase your investment return.

And this demonstrates the value of investing in stocks for the long term. The longer the compounding continues, the richer you get.

Look at the brain teaser example. If the boy had chosen February (with only 28 days), he would have received nearly 8 million dollars less. What he received on Day 29 and Day 30 was more than the rest of the month combined.

Another reason to invest in stocks for the long term, and compound your investments by reinvesting your income from them, is there will be times (such as now, as I write) when stocks are in a bear market.

When that happens, rejoice!

Chapter 9

Be Grateful for Bear Markets

Because it gives you the chance to buy the shares of companies cheap.

Right now we're in a bear market. Some people think the stock market is going to go down a lot more, and some people think it will soon go back up.

I don't know who is right.

But I do know stocks of good companies are a lot cheaper now than they were back in 2007.

If you have a job and can afford to buy stock, buy as much as you can (but finish reading this book first, so you know what to buy).

I once heard my grandfather—who had a good job throughout the 1930s—complain he could have gotten rich during the Great Depression because he wanted to buy stocks then while they were so cheap, but his wife was afraid and prevented him.

Do you think I—as one of his heirs—wish he'd gotten fabulously wealthy? (err…yes!)

I realize a lot of people right now do not have good jobs. They're working at fast food places even after graduating from college.

Many others were working but have been laid off or cut back.

That's tough, and I wish you luck if that's the position you're in. When you are able to start investing, do so.

But if you do have the money and you're not investing in stocks, you're being foolish, because this bear market is the buying opportunity of your lifetime.

Now let's return to the basics of stock investing. The original purpose of stock exchanges was to raise money for new companies. They do so by making an Initial Public Offering (IPO).

Chapter 10

What are Initial Public Offerings (IPO)s

A big part of America's wealth comes from its culture of entrepreneurship, invention and innovation.

It comes from people having an idea for something new, or an improvement on something old, or even using someone else's innovation—as Steven Jobs used Xerox's idea of a Graphical User Interface (GUI) on personal computers.

Then working to bring that idea to the world.

There's one small problem—money.

It takes money to hire people. It takes money to pay for supplies. And to build factories. And to buy equipment. And to pay for national advertising campaigns.

And the small company started by the entrepreneur in their garage doesn't have the money necessary to expand the business.

If given a choice, I'm sure most entrepreneurs would rather keep the company private and pay for everything themselves. (So far, it's worked for Mark Zuckerman and Facebook)

However, most do not have that choice. They must obtain more money or remain small.

By selling off a part of their company, they can raise the money they need to build that new factory from stock market investors.

So they make a deal with investment bankers on Wall Street.

There are a lot of legal hurdles, paperwork requirements and so forth, but it's the job of the investment banker to guide the small private company to being listed on a stock exchange.

The company must meet the requirements of the stock exchange, which doesn't want low quality companies.

It must also meet higher accounting and disclosure standards set by the Securities and Exchange Commission. This is a big step. Private companies don't have to reveal their numbers to anybody except the IRS.

Public companies are required to be very open and transparent about their businesses. That's for the protection of us investors.

IPOs also require a team of very expensive lawyers.

In a typical arrangement, the company's owners and original investors will own a large chunk of the shares of stock. Brokerage houses on Wall Street will have some to sell to their customers.

A public relations firm will do its best to "sell" the company's bright future to stock brokers and the general public.

When everything is ready, a date is set.

When the market opens, the shares of stock are for sale.

Sometimes there is a frantic rush for them, and the price goes up tremendously.

Sometimes the demand is lower than expected. In the past few years, some planned IPOs have been cancelled due to a lack of interest from investors.

This process is also archaic and inefficient, designed to make Wall Street investment bankers and lawyers wealthy at the expense both of buyers of the IPO stock (who pay too much money) and the newly listed company (which receives too little money).

It's likely in the future a more efficient Dutch auction IPO process, such as Google had, will become the norm. But right now the financial industry is resisting that trend.

That's the basic purpose of having a stock exchange.

Should you buy brand new IPO shares of stock?

First of all, unless you become one of your broker's favorite customers, you probably won't get the opportunity. Those shares are reserved for customers who have made the broker a lot of money (Which, by the way, is bad for your portfolio. Being loved by a stockbroker is not quite as bad as being loved by a casino, but it's close.)

Historically, IPOs as a whole have a poor record.

Yes, every successful customer started out with an IPO, and if you'd bought Microsoft or Wal-Mart and so on at the beginning, and held on to them, you'd have made a lot of money.

But you can't know the winners from the losers in advance.

By now you may be wondering what that has to do with the ordinary buying and selling of shares that goes on every business day.

Chapter 11

What Happens at a Stock Exchange

People and institutions buy and sell stock.

After a company has held its IPO, its stock is available for sale on what's called the secondary market.

That just means you can no longer buy the stock directly from the company's representatives (as during the IPO), but you can buy it from anyone who is willing to sell at your price.

To do that you give the buy order to your broker. If you have it and want to sell it, you give the sell order to your broker, and they arrange for someone to buy it.

Technically, this ability to buy and sell every business day of the week is not required to raise money for new businesses.

If you really believe in the future of a new company, why not just buy some of its stock at the IPO and hold it forever?

Because people are people, and will want to sell the stock—in a few days, a few years or a few decades.

After all, what good is owning shares of stock of a business if you can't get any cash out of them? Cash is what you need to pay your bills with.

Plus, sometimes people are faced with unexpected emergencies.

Today you have money available to buy some IPO stock. Next month your son needs a liver transplant, or you and your wife decide to go on a world cruise.

If people could not easily buy and sell the shares of stock they own, they'd be reluctant to buy IPO shares of stock, and new companies would find it a lot more difficult to raise the cash they need to expand.

Besides, good IPO stock shares are often made available only to a broker's favorite customers. Why shouldn't the common herd (us), get to buy IPO stock a week or two later?

But isn't this constant buying and selling a kind of gambling? Isn't that what's so bad about modern Wall Street? That so many people are buying and selling without a clue about the companies?

Chapter 12

Isn't Stock Speculation a Problem for the Economy?

I know from comments posted to one of my videos on YouTube some people think the stock market used to serve the good purpose of raising money for companies, but now it's a giant casino and damaging the economy because people are just trying to use it to get rich.

The truth is, the stock market has always been—and still is—BOTH.

Nowadays people can hook themselves up to the stock exchanges, monitor the action on their computers and buy and sell with the click of a mouse. Many of them are day traders.

This means they may buy a stock expecting it to go up in the next five minutes, and they then sell.

Win or lose, they close out all their positions at the end of the day.

Some people make some big money at this, but most lose their shirts. It takes some real talent to figure out the short term market (or extremely good luck).

Unless you have a 100% accurate crystal ball or sixth sense of the future, I strongly advise you to stay far away from day trading.

A lot of sensible people criticize day trading, and they're right.

What some people are wrong about is it's nothing new.

From the 1870s to the 1920s the United States had many bucket shops, when people basically placed bets on the prices of stocks. The bucket shop owner was in contact with the market through a telephone line or ticker tape machine.

These bucket shop operations didn't affect the market itself, because the bets were made with the bucket shop owner. It was not actually buying and selling stock. But the participants made or lost money based on their opinions of the stocks rising and falling.

That's how a famous trader from those old days, Jesse Livermore, got started.

There were also people who hung around brokerages during the hours the New York Stock Exchange was open, and bought and sold stock.

In the 1920s lots of people speculated on stocks, more so than now, because they could buy on 10% margin.

Buying on margin means they did not pay the full price of the stock.

In the 1920s it was legal to pay just 10%. For the other 90% you borrowed money from your broker (who charged you a market rate of interest).

So long as the stock's price kept going up, you were making big money. But when it started to go down, you could quickly lose all your equity in the stock.

There's no doubt 10% margin buying created a lot of speculative buying on Wall Street in the 1920s. And, when the bubble started to burst, this buying on margin contributed to the overwhelming size of the crash.

Today, it's against the law for brokers to let you buy stock with less than 50% margin.

I strongly advise you do not to buy on margin at all. There is no benefit. It is risky, and even if the stock goes up as you hope it will, you have to pay the interest on the money you borrowed from your broker, which is an unnecessary expense. Plus, to get permission to buy on margin, you'll have to fill out an application that will want to know your entire financial history.

The lesson to draw from this:

1. Greedy stock speculators are nothing new.

2. It's okay to be greedy, but don't be a stock speculator. It doesn't work unless you're incredibly lucky.

3. Don't buy on margin

So what kinds of stocks are available for investment?

Chapter 13

Kinds of Stocks

Stocks can be categorized in many ways.

One of the most common is by size of the company.

The word "cap" here is short for capitalization. That is the total value of all the company's outstanding stock.

If the company has 2 billion shares outstanding selling for $6 per share, its market capitalization or market "cap" is $12 billion and so it's considered a large cap stock.

The numbers aren't set in stone, but you get the basic idea.

1. Small cap—$300 million to $2 billion

2. Mid cap—$2 to $10 billion

3. Large cap—over $10 billion

Stocks are also categorized by the industry the company is in. Similar companies are grouped into sectors.

Common sectors include:

Utilities

Basic Materials

Conglomerates

Consumer Goods

Financial

Healthcare

Industrial Goods

Services

Technology

Real Estate Investment Trusts

Energy

Transportation

I think the most useful way to categorize stocks is by whether or not they pay dividends.

If it doesn't pay dividends, it's a "growth" stock, because growth in the company and its share price would be the only reason to buy it.

What are dividends?

I'm glad you asked…

Chapter 14

What are Dividends?

Dividends are payments of money the company sends out to its shareholders.

Normally in the US, companies send out dividends on a quarterly dividend schedule, but that's not an obligation. In the rest of the world, dividends are sent when the company wants to send them.

In the US sometimes companies send out only a one-time or special dividend payment, but don't normally pay the usual quarterly dividends.

Many companies choose not to pay dividends.

Dividends must be approved by the company's Board of Directors. They vote to pay a certain amount of money for every outstanding share of stock.

They also determine the ex-dividend date. That's the date BEFORE which you must be an owner of the stock to qualify to receive dividends.

If you buy the stock on or after the ex-dividend date, you won't receive that dividend distribution.

It takes time to make sure the cash is in the bank, access the database of shareholders, print up the checks and envelopes, mail them etc. A line has to be drawn somewhere. The ex-dividend date is that line.

If you want those dividends, you must buy the stock no later than the day before the ex-dividend date.

You may also see mention of a "record date," which is two days after the ex-dividend date.

That's because when you buy a stock, it takes three days for the sale to be settled and recorded.

Therefore, if you buy that stock the day before the ex-dividend date, that sale won't be recorded until two days after the ex-dividend date, the record date.

As a practical matter, this is not something you should need to spend time thinking about. Once you buy some stock, you'll start receiving dividends with the next distribution and continue receiving them so long as you own the stock.

Where Does the Cash for Dividends Come From?

Of course it comes out of the profits the company is making. If it's not profitable, it shouldn't be paying any dividends.

Make no mistake—this cash is money the company could keep and use for some business purpose, such as building a new factory in Thailand or even buying up an annoying competitor.

For this reason, relatively new companies which are not well established, which have a lot of competition, which must continuously spend money to keep up with the latest technological advances—rarely pay dividends.

The high tech sector is typical.

Microsoft's IPO was in 1986, but it didn't begin paying a dividend until

2004.

So generally, companies paying dividends are older and well-established in their industries.

There are some sectors where it's expected companies pay dividends if they can (Utilities) and some sectors where they're required to by law (Real Estate Investment Trusts and Master Limited Partnerships).

The right to receive dividends (if they are declared by the Board of Directors) is one of the benefits of owning the company's stock.

Remember, as a stockholder you are an owner. You are a partner. Your liability is limited to the amount you paid for your shares. You don't have to do any work (unless you are also an employee of the company), but you get to share in its profits.

There's a Terrific Long-Term Benefit to Dividends

They generally go up over time.

I've mentioned Microsoft. It was paying 8 cents per share per quarter in 2004. In December 2011 it paid 20 cents per share per quarter.

In seven years the income you get from owning Microsoft stock has gone up 250%.

Have Social Security, pensions or average wages gone up 250% in the past seven years?

You know the answer to that one—heck no. Social Security checks have been "frozen" since 2009 and most employed people consider themselves lucky if their paychecks haven't been cut.

For a longer term perspective, from 1955 to 2007, the shares of Hershey my mother bought went from paying 55 cents per one share per quarter to $35.70 per 1955 share. Thanks to stock splits, one 1955 share is now 120 shares, and each pays 29 3/4 cents per share.

Now, I need to add here that this is not guaranteed. Many companies don't raise their dividends every year, though some companies have a long record of raising them every year. In bad times (such as the current financial crisis/recession) dividends can be cut or even eliminated altogether.

If given a choice between paying dividends and putting the company's existence in jeopardy, a responsible Board of Directors will choose to keep the cash.

Therefore, it's a good idea to put the odds of getting annual dividend raises in your favor. We'll cover that in a future chapter.

For now, we need to know how to invest in stocks.

Chapter 15

Ways to Invest in Stocks

The main ways are:

I. Individual Company Shares

This is the most obvious way to invest in stocks.

You simply tell your broker you want 100 shares of Microsoft, 200 shares of Coca-Cola or whatever company you want.

Advantages: it's simple and easy. If the company pays dividends, they are sent right to you or into your brokerage account. You pay an upfront commission to your broker for the service of buying the stock for you, but after that there are no expenses. (And you can minimize the commission by using a discount broker instead of an old-fashioned full-service one.)

Disadvantages: if that company goes bankrupt, you lose your entire investment. After the lawyers and bondholders are done, you'll get little or nothing.

The company may not go out of business, but it could have problems and go down in price even when the economy is good, the sun is shining, and its competitors are breaking profitability records.

Also, if you're investing a small amount out of your paychecks, it'd be expensive to pay a commission every week or two, just to buy a few shares.

(But you can get around that disadvantage by letting paycheck deductions accumulate until you have enough cash to buy 100 shares of the stock you want to buy.)

II. Mutual Funds

Mutual funds are where investors pool their funds so they can buy a wide variety of stocks.

There are two kinds:

1. Actively traded

2. Index

Actively traded mutual funds are the normal kind, what people generally are referring to when they discuss mutual funds.

To open an account you hand your money over to the mutual fund (many require minimums of from $2-5,000). The mutual fund manager uses your money—and that of all other account holders—to buy a portfolio of stocks they believe will go up in price more than the market.

When those stocks go up, so does the value of your mutual fund shares.

When those stocks go down, so does the value of your mutual fund shares.

Advantages: You can make small deposits through payroll deduction without being charged a commission.

You get a lot more diversification than you could otherwise afford.

Disadvantages: It would take a lot longer book to fully describe the disadvantages.

Many mutual funds charge you upfront or backend fees or loads. These can be as high as 7%. That means if you invest $100,000 in a mutual fund, you get $93,000 worth of shares. The other $7,000 goes into the pockets of the company.

Why any investor tolerates this, I don't know. The one thing I'd praise the mainstream financial media for is warning the investing public against mutual funds that charge loads. They've done a good job of that, but despite all their efforts, many people still pay these loads.

One reason is many people buy mutual funds through their brokers, and the mutual fund company pays the broker a commission out of that load. This is a waste of your money. You cannot buy Walt Disney stock yourself on the stock exchange, so you need a broker for that, and they deserve that relatively commission.

But you don't need a broker to call up a mutual fund's 800 number or visit their website and open your account. So you don't need to pay a broker to do that for you.

The mutual fund company and manager do not work for free. They have to pay service representatives to staff their 800 number customer service number. They have to print and mail your statements. They have to take out full page ads in the mainstream financial ads so they keep growing the fund. They have to pay commissions every time they buy and sell stocks. They expect 7 or 8 (or 9!) figure bonuses.

All that money comes out of the fund—which is partly your money.

The manager works hard to find the best stocks to buy. So hard, in fact, studies have proven on the average they UNDER-perform the market by around 1%.

That's a significant statistic, and we're going to return to this subject, but for now let's stick with mutual funds.

When they sell stocks for more than they paid, they incur capital gains taxes which YOU—and everyone else who still owns shares in the fund at the end of the year—must pay taxes on.

At any given moment you don't know what stocks the fund owns. Yes, they send out quarterly reports, but by the time you see them they're out of date. The manager has the right to buy and sell at their discretion.

They may not even be buying up the types of securities the fund claims to be about.

For instance, the manager of a small cap stock fund may buy large cap stocks because they believe large caps are going to go up more than small caps in the next few months.

Index funds are made up only of the stocks in a given index.

For example, the Vanguard S&P 500 Index Fund owns all the stocks in the S&P 500 Index, in the exact proportions of the index.

This means their expenses are a lot lower. They buy and sell stocks only if and when S&P changes the makeup of the index, which is generally infrequent. This also keeps capital gains to a minimum.

That also means they do not underperform the market, because they are the market.

If the market goes up, so does their share price. If the market goes down, so does their share price.

This could be called a disadvantage as well, because index funds never go up higher than the market.

III. Exchange Traded Funds (EFT)s

Exchange Traded Funds aren't quite 20 years old, and they're relatively unknown to ordinary investors, especially compared to mutual funds, but they're rapidly gaining in popularity.

The basic format of an ETF is for the company to raise money through issuing shares of stock—an IPO.

However, their "product" is simply their promise to use that money to buy shares of stock in a particular index.

The first and still the most popular ETF holds the stocks of the S&P 500 Index. Its acronym is Standard & Poor's Depositary Receipts, SPDR for short, or "Spiders" when speaking.

When you own 100 shares of Spiders, you own a representative fraction of the entire S&P 500.

After the IPO, the ETF's shares are bought and sold on the secondary market just like shares of stock.

If you want to buy an ETF, you tell your broker to buy some. You never contact the ETF company the way you would a mutual fund company.

But that's also a good thing. ETF expenses are lower than a mutual fund's because they don't mail out statements, or staff 800 number lines, or continually buy or sell shares of stock because customers buy and sell shares.

You get the same market performance and diversification as you do with index funds. You don't pay for ETF company staffing.

The value of your ETF shares depends on the value of the index. When it goes up, your ETF's market value goes up, and it goes down if the index's market price goes down.

The one big disadvantage of ETFs is, just as with individual stocks, you can't afford to pay a commission every time you get a paycheck. But you can let that money accumulate, then buy 100 shares of an ETF when you have the money available.

Some brokerages do allow no-commission automatic reinvestment of dividends from stocks and ETFs.

If you've guessed by now I favor Exchange Traded Funds, you'd be right. However, the choices available to you depend on how you're investing.

Chapter 16

How to Invest in Stocks

There are two basic kinds of stock accounts: taxable and nontaxable/tax-deferred.

A taxable account is one you open up either at a brokerage or a mutual fund. You have to pay the taxes you incur.

Brokerages are companies (one person or covering the entire nation) which will buy and sell stocks and other securities for you. They'll hold them for you as well. And they'll send you money when you ask for it.

Traditionally, people used stock brokers in their local areas. Nowadays I recommend you use an online broker so you can do most of your business at home at your computer.

Here's a list from Wikipedia:

http://en.wikipedia.org/wiki/Category:Online_brokerages

My broker is on that list. In my area (St Louis), they also have many local offices, so it's convenient for me to go there if I have a need to. But to give trading orders, I do that online.

Shop around. Check out their commissions. There's no point in paying more than you have to. A few dollars may not seem like much, but all money that leaves your account is money not accumulating for your retirement. Contact them online or in person. They'll explain the paperwork they need from you.

For mutual funds, contact them directly through their 800 number or website. At your request they'll send you an application and a prospectus. Send in your money and you're on your way.

Tax-deferred (and nontaxable Roth IRAs):

In 1974 the US government passed an innovative, terrific law authorizing the creation of Individual Retirement Accounts (IRA)s.

The basic idea is you can invest a certain amount of your earned income (wages or self-employment), and let it grow, without paying taxes on that money until you withdraw it when you're old enough.

I know other countries have adopted the basic idea: Registered Retirement Savings Plan (RRSP) (Canada); Superannuation in Australia; and Individual Savings Account (ISA) (United Kingdom).

I don't know any of the details of those programs, so you if you are outside the US you'll have to check your country's laws.

Now the basic IRA concept has branched out:

401(k) plans—people working for private companies

Thrift Savings Plan—federal employees

403(b)—people working for nonprofit organizations

Keogh, Simplified Employee Pension (SEP) and SEP IRA accounts—for the self-employed

There are also Roth IRAs where you have to pay the taxes on your contribution, but you'll never be forced to withdraw it in the future. Thus it's perfect for people who wish to pay on a large inheritance.

This book is not intended to educate you on all the details of these various plans.

It's just to let you know your options.

You can open up an IRA, Keogh, SEP IRA or Roth IRA account at a broker or with a mutual fund.

401(k), the Thrift Savings Plan and 403(b) plans are all related to your workplace and controlled by your employer.

If you work for the federal government, you've probably been informed of the Thrift Savings Plan. If you haven't enrolled, you should. You can have up to 10% of your paycheck withheld and invested for you. The government matches the first 5%. Therefore, if you're not having that 5% withheld from your paycheck, you're throwing away free money from the government! It's an easy way to immediately double your money.

Unless you plan to retire within the next 10 years, you should put all your money into the C plan, which is basically an S&P 500 Index fund. Stocks are cheap now. Buy them up.

If you work for a nonprofit organization, see if they have a 403(b) plan available for you. I can't tell you what your options will be.

If you work for a private company, check to see whether there is a 401(k) plan available. Your options will vary with the company you're with.

In general, if you qualify for "matching" of funds from your employer— take it!

That's where your employer matches some or all of what you put into the fund.

It's possible you will have the option to invest in the stock of your company and/or a variety of mutual funds.

Investing in your company's stock is generally considered a bad idea because if your company goes downhill in the future, you could lose both your job and your retirement funds. If you're too young to remember Enron, search online for the clips of that company's ex-employees bemoaning the loss of their jobs and their retirement fund's stock. It was heartbreaking.

On the other hand, the employees of successful companies have used stock purchases to make themselves wealthy. I remember reading in the 1990s even the administrative aides at Dell were millionaires.

You may be sure your employer is one of the good ones, and I hope you're right—but until the news of the fraud broke, Enron's employees thought their company was in great shape.

You are allowed to have as many of these retirement accounts as you qualify for.

For example: you have a 401(k) plan on your job. You put the maximum you're allowed into it. You can also go to a broker or mutual fund and open up an IRA or Roth IRA, then put in the IRA maximum.

And if you have a business as well as that job, you can open up a retirement account for the self-employed.

One other suggestion: unless you're close to retirement now, you're going to change employers (voluntarily or involuntarily) sometime in the future. When that happens, transfer your work-related tax-deferred account to an IRA or Roth IRA at a brokerage.

Then you can buy whatever stocks or ETFs you wish with it.

If you keep that money in an account with an ex-employer, you're out of the loop about what's happening there. Plus, if you die, the law would make your heirs pay some unnecessary taxes. If it's in your own IRA, you have a lot more options and can leave it to your heirs.

What if you don't have the money to open a brokerage or mutual fund account?

There's a great way for investors starting out small.

Chapter 17

Dividend Re-Investment Plans— DRIPs

There is one alternative way to invest in stocks if you don't have enough money for a brokerage or mutual fund account.

Dividend Re-Investment Plans or DRIPs

You basically open an account with a major company that pays regular quarterly dividends. You can start with some of these for a very low amount.

They use your money to buy as many shares as it buys, based on the market price—even if that's a fractional share.

For instance, if their stock price is $100 per share and you start with $50, you'll own 1/2 of a share.

But they won't charge you a brokerage commission.

And when it comes time to dividends, they'll give you credit for your dividend based on how many shares you own. And they'll reinvest that automatically.

Let's say this company is paying 20 cents per share this quarter.

You own 1/2 of a share, so you get 10 cents.

But of course they won't send you a check, they'll use it to buy a tiny fraction of a share, so next quarter you'll have slightly more than 1/2 of a share, and therefore earn a slighter higher dividend, etc.

Obviously, at these small amounts of money we're not talking about getting rich quick.

My advice is: open up a DRIP account. When you can afford to add more money to it, do so. Otherwise, forget you own it.

Don't touch it until you retire.

You'll be pleasantly surprised.

Here's a list of some DRIPs available:

https://www-us.computershare.com/investor/plans/buyshares. asp?stype=nof

Now how do you figure out which companies are in good financial shape?

Actually you can't, but you should still be familiar with the basic of company accounting statements. It's not too hard—really.

Chapter 18

Basic Company Financial Documents

Some stock market experts advise you to "analyze" a company's financial statements before you buy its stock.

Unless you're an experienced stock analyst or accountant in that industry, I think that's poor advice.

For one thing, if a company is fraudulent, it will hide the evidence off the record. Enron is the classic example of this. You could have analyzed its balance sheets until the cows came home without finding all the off-book structures it was using. If the accountants auditing a company's books can't or won't find fraud, how will you?

However, I do believe it's a good idea for everybody to know the basics of corporate financial statements.

You don't have to know a debit from a credit, but two financial statements are very important:

I. The Income Statement

Income - Expenses = Net Profit

Income is all the money a business takes in.

Expenses is the category for all the money the company must spend or set aside to generate that income. Salaries, rent, depreciation, and so on.

The higher the "Net Profit" the better.

Although I doubt the ability of ordinary investors (including myself even though I have a degree in accounting) to analyze the Income Statement in detail, I can advise you not to invest in any company with a NEGATIVE bottom line figure. That's a loss, not a profit.

Sounds like common sense, but in the late 1990s a lot of people bought stocks in dot com companies that were losing money.

II. Balance Statement

This is a little harder to show and explain.

As traditionally presented, it's in two columns.

The left column consists of the value of all the company's assets: cash, equipment, factories, trademarks, accounts receivable, inventory in stock, and so on.

For the sake of an example, let's say it's $10 million.

The right column is in two parts.

The top part consists of what the company owes: accounts payable, salaries not yet paid, long term bonds, short term bank loans, and so on.

Let's say it's $4 million.

The third part is the difference between assets and liabilities:

Assets - Liabilities = Net Equity

$10 million - $4 million = $6 million

If the company has 1 million shares of stock outstanding, each share's "book" value is $6.

$6 million / 1 million = $6

Frankly, any company can manipulate its figures to make itself look good on paper. Some don't have to because they're doing well honestly. Some have too much integrity. Some can do so while remaining within Generally Accepted Accounting Principles (GAAP). Some GAAP guidelines are arguably too loose, so a company can abide by them and still be "spinning" the numbers to make themselves look good.

Depending on how clever they are, it may well take an experienced accountant with access to original records and experience in that industry (because norms in industries vary a lot) to figure out the truth.

You and I don't have the resources to accomplish this.

That's another reason I say buying individual stocks is too risky.

It's also another reason to invest for dividends.

Companies that pay dividends may have problems they're covering up, but they're able to come up with the cash to pay those dividends, and that's something.

We're almost ready to buy some stocks, but first maybe you want to know who determines what stock market prices are.

Chapter 19

Why Stock Prices Go Up and Down

I know from seeing online questions there is some confusion regarding this issue—and it's a very important one—so let's start here.

If you know anything about economics, you may have heard of the Law of Supply and Demand.

The greater the demand for something, the higher its price.

The greater the supply of something, the lower its price.

This is most obvious at auctions.

Ever been to an auction where the auctioneer was trying to sell something only one or two people wanted?

The price stays low. One person bids the minimum, nobody raises, and that's the end of it.

But if there are ten people who REALLY want that antique/painting/coin/stamp/comic book, they keep raising the price on each other until it's sky-high.

Now go to eBay and check out the prices of Harry Potter books. Sure, they're popular, but that just means millions have been sold, and eBay has hundreds of them available. The auction owners will be lucky to get a few bucks for them, just because there are so many for sale there.

It's the same with stocks. "Supply" is not usually an issue (except perhaps for some very small companies which have only a few thousand shares of stock outstanding), but in the stock market "demand" can go up and down a lot.

During the high tech, dot com boom of 1995-99, everybody and his dog was buying any and every stock that even had a website. Many were only websites. Demand was very high.

As the most well-known tech stock, in those five years Microsoft surged from under $5 to just under $60—and that was tame compared to Yahoo! (It was a crazy time.)

Sometimes the emotion runs the other way. On "Black Monday"— October 19, 1987—the stock market as a whole lost around 22% of its value. Everybody panicked at once, and so everybody was selling.

When everybody is selling, nobody is left to buy, and so prices go down.

As I write this in December 2011, the overall market is down, though not so dramatically as Black Monday. But at around 12,000 the market is still substantially down from its October 2007 high of over 14,000.

A "bull" market is one where prices are generally going up.

A "bear" market is officially where prices are generally down at least 20% from their high.

By that definition, we're still in the bear market that began when the market went below its 14,000 peak in October 2007.

However, because the market is up a lot since its March 2009 bottom of below 7,000, the mainstream financial media is calling it a bull market.

In my opinion, the mainstream financial media is deceptive.

Some describe market prices as a tug of war between the bulls (people who are buying because they believe the market price is going up) and bears (people who are selling because they believe the market price is going down).

So it still comes down to demand.

When more people are buying a stock, the price goes up.

When more people are selling a stock, the price goes down.

It's a war between greed and fear.

When there's a bull market such as 1995-99, people buy at ever higher prices because they believe they can later sell at an even higher price, and they're greedy for this profit.

When there's a bear market, people keep selling because they're afraid prices are going to go even lower, and they want to get out now while they can still get something for their stock. They're scared of losing more money.

In the final analysis, the answer to the question of who determines market prices is us—all investors as a whole.

Of course, you don't and can't control other investors. You have all you can do to control yourself.

The same battle between greed and fear is fought in the mind and heart of every investor.

I can't fight it for you. My job with this book is to give you the facts you need to invest rationally, without either greed or fear.

Both can lead you to make serious mistakes.

Just as with corporations, it's easy to talk or write about the "stock market" as something alive and conscious, a separate entity unto itself.

However, just as with corporations, the stock market is composed of people – many people.

And we all know people are emotional.

In the short run, the stock market is extremely volatile.

Chapter 20

Stock Market Volatility

In Chapter 4 we went over what determines stock prices, and figured out it comes down to a war between fear and greed.

Look at a long term chart of the Dow Jones Average, such as this one:

http://stockcharts.com/freecharts/historical/djia1900.html

Your eyes should immediately notice two things, both extremely important, obvious and—in the long term—surprisingly reassuring.

Since 1900 the Dow has gone up a large amount. The picture looks like the slope of a steep mountain.

The line going up is jagged.

Yes, it has gone up a lot in the past 111 years, but there have been a few VERY steep drops. Look at August 1929 to 1932, for example.

This is known as volatility. Stock market prices can go up a lot—and down a lot.

From October 2007 the Dow went from a peak just over 14,000 to just below 7,000 in March 2009.

That's an over 50% decline in just 17 months.

Personal finance experts are fond of telling you how the stock market goes up an average of about 10% per year, so if you just invest so much per year, by the time you're 65 you'll have X million bucks.

This is both true and deceptive.

Historically, on average, the stock market has gone up an average of about 10% per year.

That's an AVERAGE.

Some years it's gone up a lot more than that, some years a lot less. Some years it's been boring and barely budged.

Also, that 10% average is a PAST average.

The government requires people selling investing systems to advise you "past performance does not guarantee future performance."

That's a phrase you should engrave into your mind. They are most likely the truest words ever written by a government agency.

Nobody knows what the stock market's future average will be. Not until the future has become the past and we're looking back and calculating it, and by then it'll be too late for you to profit from it.

The experts often tell you although the stock market is volatile, you should invest for the long term.

I agree with that, but they forget to mention you can invest diligently throughout your working career, but if a powerful, long term bear market begins right as you retire, you won't live the lifestyle you've been dreaming of.

Just ask anyone who retired in 2007.

This tendency of the stock market to go up and down is called "risk" by the stock experts.

I prefer to call it simply volatility, because to me "risk" means "danger," and that's not same as stock prices go up or down.

The stock market as a whole is not very risky in the long run (you can see the graph's trend is strongly upward), but individual stocks are.

That's because under capitalism business will also seek to make a profit by providing goods and services, and the stock market makes that easier.

However, individual companies can—and do—fail.

That's real risk.

But with stock market prices jumping around so much—even from minute to minute—how can stock investors know the true value of a share of stock?

Chapter 21

How to Determine a Stock's "True" Value

This is the crucial factor in "beating" the stock market.

I've seen people asking how to do this on Yahoo Answers, LinkedIn and other places.

I had to wonder, are they simple-minded?

After all, if anybody really knows how to "beat" the stock market, that's the key to trillions of dollars.

Why in the world would they just give it to you on Yahoo Answers?

To think they would is so tremendously naive I was overcome with shock when I first saw it.

Then I realized, the person asking is probably very smart.

They're used to winning.

They're like a few of the girls I used to go to school with.

They carried all their books home every night and studied each one every night. They did all their homework on time. They listened carefully to the teacher during class time. They did their required readings. They were never caught unprepared by pop quizzes. They over-prepared for their midterms and finals. They got solid As they thoroughly earned.

They were always at the top of grading curve. Their only competition was each other.

They played by the rules. I've no doubt they went through college the same way and got good grades and are now working at responsible jobs making good (though not tremendous) money.

Their younger versions are growing up online, so it's only natural for them, when faced with the need to begin investing, to want to learn the rules or techniques to beat the market. Just as they learned the rules for Chemistry and Geometry, they want to learn the rules for beating the stock market.

And then they plan to apply them just as diligently as they did their homework assignments and therefore make straight As in Real Life Investing just as they did in Algebra and Biology in high school.

Too bad real life doesn't work that way.

For one thing, there is NO "one way" everybody agrees to value stocks.

If that were true, the stock market would be very boring. Stocks wouldn't be bought or sold except at the price "everybody" agreed was right. And then why buy or sell?

For another thing, it's possible for millions of kids to get an "A" in the same subject in high schools all across America.

The stock exchanges are not isolated into small groups.

You're not competing with just 29 other kids, 95% of whom don't work half as hard as you do. You're competing against many of the best minds in the world, around the world. Math and Finance PhDs from Harvard and MIT, backed up by banks of super computer networks monitoring the world's financial markets in real time, with databases of all stock prices in recorded history, operating with software based on proprietary formulas.

You're competing against hedge funds, pension funds, mutual funds, life insurance companies, trading firms and others who have their own sophisticated ways of analyzing the markets, looking for price disparities they can take advantage of.

When a trading opportunity comes along, the software puts in the order. Asking a person to make the decision would take too long. The opportunity would vanish by the time they could analyze the data.

How do you get an "A" in this class?

People who claim they can beat the market must have some method of calculating how much a stock is "really" worth, so they can compare that to the market price.

If the stock is "really" worth more than its current market price, it's a buy.

If the stock is "really" worth the same as its current market price, ignore it.

If the stock is "really" worth less than its current market price, sell it (if you already own it).

There are three commonly accepted techniques to accomplish this:

1. Fundamental Analysis

Fundamental analysis attempts to evaluate a company's stock by analyzing the company's business. It's the logical place to start.

Compute the company's financial reports and ratios such as the ever-popular P/E ratio.

That's Price (per share of stock) divided by Earnings (per share of stock).

Some analysts also look at the Price to Sales and Price to Book Value ratios.

Debt to Equity is important for determining whether or not the company is over-leveraged. That is, whether or not it owes too much money. Almost all companies owe some money. Some have little or no long term debt, which makes them much more likely to survive hard times such as the current recession.

On the other hand, and this is particularly true in boom times, not owing money can limit a company's profits.

Therefore, analysts compare a company to others in the same industry.

Figure out where the company stands in its industry. How good are its products and services? Are they in demand by customers?

How well are its products selling? At what point are they in the product lifecycle—still new and trendy or boring and old hat?

Is the company or a leader or a laggard? Is it capital intensive (that is, dependent on lots of expensive machinery, such as a microchip manufacturing plant) or mainly a paper business (such as insurance).

How well do its products fit in with social trends? Do consumers want what they're selling?

You must also figure out how good its upper management is. This can be trickier than is commonly acknowledged. Some managers have good track records, but for some reason don't pan out at another company.

Some people look at the company's return on equity. The higher the net income per share of stock, the better the company is performing.

Some people prefer to look at only the company or the industry. Many others look at the overall economy. Good times or a recession? What are interest rates?

The company may be affected by international events. Is it dependent on political conditions in South America? Shipping delays in Asia?

If that sounds like a lot of work with uncertain results for someone who's not an expert in that industry, you're correct. It is.

And as mentioned before, if the company is misrepresenting or actually falsifying figures, you have no way of knowing that.

2. Technical Analysis

This does not really analyze and compare stock prices. It does look at the chart of the stock's recent prices and volume. It determines from the shape of the chart and other factors whether in the near future the stock's price is going to go up, down, or sideways.

Some chart patterns include "head and shoulders," double top or bottom, flag, pennants, cup and handle, and many more.

They also look at the price's moving average, relative strength index, advance/decline ratio, relative strength index, short interest, Fibonacci ratios and more.

Some technical analysts have other techniques. Candlestick charting uses techniques from 17th century rice markets in Japan.

Some varieties of technical analysis, such as Elliot Wave Theory, look for cycles of repeating patterns.

Some of what technicians say makes some sense, but interpreting the chart patterns can be quite subjective.

Besides, the more people look at the charts, the more likely it is any value from them will be gone—bought up by others—before you can place the order with your broker.

3. Momentum Investing

These people focus on a stock's price. If it's been going up, they say, it'll keep going up (until it stops, whenever that may be).

Many momentum investors look at the charts. They generally don't invest in a stock until its price has broken through a "line of resistance." That is, historically it hasn't gone above a certain price, and suddenly it does.

Then, they believe, it will probably keep going.

Sometimes it does. Sometimes it falls back to a lower price.

All of these systems are short-term. They are attempting to predict what the stock's price will do in the near future.

The most logical system is called "Value" investing.

Chapter 22

Value or Contrarian Investing

This concept seems brain-dead obvious.

Find a stock that's underpriced and buy it.

Wait for the market to "discover its mistake," so the price goes to its "correct" valuation, then sell.

The original "god" of value investing was Benjamin Graham, who said it's simply paying $1 to get $1.50, and if you can't see the value of that, you're an idiot (he put it more politely, but that's the gist of it).

One of his examples was a company he found that, in addition to its main business, owned a rock quarry. The market was correctly pricing the company's stock for its main business, but ignoring the value of the rock quarry, so he bought the stock.

I can't resist pointing out Graham's heyday as a stock picker and analyst was during the 1930s, when the entire stock market was had a "Fire Sale" sign on it.

Graham's most famous student (the only one to get an "A" in Graham's college course) is the famous Warren Buffett.

Early in his investing career, Buffett found his own "rock quarry." A company that made windmills of all things, was sitting on a big block of cash. Buffett bought enough to sit on the Board of Directors—where the others voted down every suggestion he made for putting that cash to use. He wound up selling the stock.

Paying $1 for $1.50 isn't so great if you can't spend the $1.50.

In some ways, this method requires some arrogance. It means you have to feel confident you can locate value nobody else—even those funds with banks of supercomputers and supergeek "quants" (the nickname for people who apply sophisticated quantitative analysis to picking stocks) analyzing the market—has found.

Remember how market prices go up and down.

If people think a stock is underpriced, they're going to buy, driving up the price until it reaches what they believe the "real" worth to be. When it reaches that price, they stop buying.

So if a given stock at $44 is really worth $50, it would already be selling for $50.

Now, Buffett has done pretty well for himself. Most people say it's because he picks stocks that beat the market. Some of his picks do, others don't.

I suspect it's because he likes to buy stocks that pay good dividends (such as Coca-Cola) and entire companies with good cash flow.

You and I can do the first, but not the second.

However, there are those who claim the market is too efficient to put $1.50 on sale for only $1.00.

Chapter 23

The Efficient Market Theory

The Efficient Market Theory claims the stock market is impossible to beat in the long run because it's too efficient.

All publicly known information about a company is already reflected in its stock price.

Sure, "inside" information about a company could mean its price should be higher or lower, but trading on inside information is illegal.

Therefore, a stock's current price is the correct one.

Yes, it changes, based as new information becomes available, because of that new information.

Therefore, the ups and downs of stock prices and the market as a whole are random—they go back and forth like a drunkard.

There is a steady upward trend (remember the stock chart) because the stock market reflects the economy, and the US (and the world) is getting wealthier over time (though not in a straight line).

I'm not so sure the stock market is "efficient," and I'm not clear on how every investor somehow magically knows everything about every company, and it's also been proven the stock market is not completely random.

The market has had days of extreme movement. Sometimes they're up, sometimes they're down. But there have been far too many of them to say the market is always random in the normal statistical definition of that term.

Most days, yes. But sometimes there're days of extreme upward or downward momentum.

I'll also add that Benjamin Graham's story of manic depressive (bipolar disorder in modern psychiatric terminology) Mr. Market does make sense.

Sometimes "Mr. Market" is manic. The sun is shining, the birds are singing, God's in Heaven and all's right with the world. Mr. Market in bulletproof, and so prices stocks as high as they can go.

This is a time when investor greed is dominant. People see and hear about their friends and neighbors getting rich in the stock market, so they start buying too. They're confident soon the stock they buy today will go up in price and they will be able to sell it to someone else for more money. (Also known as the "greater fool" theory.)

When this happens, stock prices as a whole are relatively expensive.

The late 1990s were the most recent period of manic Mr. Market.

But eventually "Mr. Market" goes to the dark, depressive side. Now Mr. Market's world has been "painted black." The sky is falling. Nothing goes right.

This is a time when investor fear is dominant. People have seen the market value of their portfolios go down. Fearing the future, they sell off their stocks. This drives the prices down further.

As I write this in December 2011, Mr. Market still has the bad case of the blues he's had since 2008, and shows no sign of recovering soon.

When this happens, stock prices as a whole are relatively inexpensive.

But it's random enough that it's unpredictable.

That's the bottom line to me.

I don't know the future, and neither does anyone else.

We can come up with good guesses, but to the degree everyone else can too, the stock market will reflect them.

Plus, things happen nobody can foresee.

The general public is allowed to access the Internet. The mortgage industry stops requiring applicants to prove their income and resources. 19 terrorists attack the United States. Greece suddenly admits it doesn't even know the size of its government budget deficit.

What wild, crazy thing will happen next?

We don't know.

We can choose to buy when "Mr. Market" is depressed, but we can't wait for that.

The conclusion of the proponents of the efficient market theory is you should invest only in a broad stock market index.

What are indexes?

Chapter 24

What are Stock Market Indexes

A stock market index is a list of stocks that represent a larger group of related stocks.

The best known stock market index is the Dow Jones Industrial Average, which is what the mainstream media refers to most of the time.

Many years ago Charles Dow thought the top 30 industrial stocks could represent the health of America's economy. Not many of the current 30 Dow stocks are "industrial" companies anymore, but collectively they do a pretty job of reflecting the economy of the US.

Dow also came up with Transportation and Utilities indexes.

The index stock market pros use to evaluate the stock market as a whole is the S&P 500 Index, the 500 largest public companies in the United States.

There are countless indexes representing every one of the world's stock markets, sectors of stocks, and many other kinds of securities.

Other important stock indexes include:

Russell 3000 - top 3,000 companies in the US

Russell 2000—the smallest 2,000 out of those companies

Wilshire 5000—top 5,000 companies in the US

Indexes are important because they provide a way—through index mutual funds and Exchange Traded Funds—for investors to own small amounts of a large number of stocks with what's called transparency. That is, so you know what you own, because the composition of indexes is public information you can look up online.

This helps investors cope with the dangers of investing in the stock market by the best method proven to eliminate risk—diversification.

Chapter 25

What is Diversification

Because almost anything can happen to any one company, financial professionals have figured out the best way to reduce risk is diversification.

This means buying as many different types of stocks as possible, in as many different sectors as possible.

If one company goes out of business (it happens), you still have many more.

If you own only one company and it goes out of business, your entire portfolio is wiped out.

In fact, the ultimate stock market diversification is to buy every stock in the market.

That's the main value of having indexes. You can buy a piece of the entire S&P 500 by investing in an S&P 500 Index mutual fund or buying shares of the SPDR Exchange Traded Fund.

Some people—who wish you to buy their system for beating the market—will tell you that this is "di-worse-ification (ha ha ha)," and it dooms you to "mediocrity."

In a sense, that's correct. Your portfolio can't "beat" the market when it

IS the market.

Take a look again at the stock market from 1900 on:

http://stockcharts.com/freecharts/historical/djia1900.html

Is THAT mediocrity?

Over time, that's fabulous wealth building.

But what about BEATING the market?

People do, don't they?

Chapter 26

Who is Beating the Market?

So I've been discussing "beating" the stock market, but…

1. We're investing for 20+ years out, because the stock market is highly volatile in the short term.

2. Nobody can predict what will happen to stocks in the next 20 years.

3. To eliminate the risk of buying individual stocks, we need to buy a broad stock index (such as the S&P 500) using either an index fund or Exchange Traded Fund.

4. Fundamental analysis seems to make sense, but gets very complicated, messy and time consuming in practice. Besides, the fundamentals of every stock are going to change in the next 20 years.

5. Technical analysis may make sense, but many technicians interpret the same charts in different ways. Besides, the charts will change in the next 20 years.

6. We're competing against millions of other investors—including full time professionals with access to all the data in the world, who hire teams of Ph.Ds.

7. The market seems to be random most of the time, though with extreme

up and down moves happening more often than mere chance. In any case, it's probably impossible to predict.

But SOMEBODY beats the market, don't they?

Plenty of people claim to do so. Plenty of people get paid to do so.

But do they?

There have been many extensive studies of the predictions—both for individual stocks and the stock market as a whole—of stock brokers, stock analysts, stock commentators, news letter editors, stock system sellers, fund managers, and everybody else who goes on the public record with their predictions.

The conclusion: the ability to "beat" the market over the long run is very rare.

Yes, some people have outstanding records, some for years at a time. But then they fall down.

It seems some people are very good at predicting what stocks will do well in certain kinds of markets, and look great...until a different kind of market comes along and smashes their picks.

Could it be people who claim to beat the market have an ulterior motive (even if they're sincere in their claims)?

You'd be amazed at how many people make more money from selling their stock market predictions than from buying stock.

Do you wish to help them fatten their bank accounts?

Chapter 27

Protect Your Money From Scams and Unnecessary Expenses

Until the mid-1970s, stock brokers were allowed to charge incredibly high commissions to buy and sell stocks for you.

However, that changed, and brokers began competing on the basis of price, until now you can find brokerages that charge under $10 to buy and sell.

For example, I pay my broker $7 per trade placed online.

To make up for the lost revenue, stockbrokers began finding ways to encourage their clients to trade more often. More frequent trades equal more commissions for the stockbroker.

Some investors have been foolish enough to give their stockbrokers the authority to make trades on their behalf.

NEVER DO THIS!

Your stockbroker does not know winning stocks from losing stocks. They just want to make more money.

Make sure they understand they have no authority to make a trade on your behalf without a clear trade order from you.

Some people have lost small fortunes because their stockbrokers bought and sold a lot of stocks in their brokerage accounts. Even though some of the stocks were winners, people's accounts were drained by paying the commissions.

It's called churning. If you ever see evidence of it in your brokerage accounts, close it out immediately and report the broker to the Securities and Exchange Commission.

Crooked stockbrokers are just one of many predators who think your money is really their money (temporarily) in your pocket.

And you can lose lots of money to honest stockbrokers, just by making too many trades in your accounts.

Numerous studies have been done on brokerage accounts. The conclusion is clear: the people with the highest brokerage accounts trade the least.

People who buy and sell, buy and sell, buy and sell, always seeking a winner and to dump losers, lose money to commissions and taxes on capital gains.

That's why I advise you to buy stocks that pay dividends and never sell them.

And to accumulate the dividends until you can afford to pay 100 more shares, then do so.

Don't buy shares every time you have a few dollars, because you'll pay too many commissions.

And what is a good way for stockbrokers to make you think you need to buy and sell a lot more?

They change their name from "stockbroker" to "financial advisor" and tell you about the great stocks you should buy.

Stock Market Gurus

Your snail mail box and your email inbox can be full of solicitations from people who want you to believe they know how to beat the market.

They use selective statistics (their copywriters document all their good calls, but leave out their bad calls), appeal to your fear and greed, swear they're on your side against the politicians and Wall Streeter, and pull every other trick in the book to make you think they're smarter than they really are, and on your side.

Some of them highlight a small stock bound to be the next Wal-Mart or Microsoft, and promise to reveal more such winners if you subscribe. If you read the fine print, you'll find that company "sponsored" the mailing. That is, they paid the newsletter to mail out the advertisement saying how great they are.

That first newsletter will probably cost $49 or $99 for a year. Then you'll get letters "upselling" you to their more expensive newsletters and services. Some of them even host cruises and conferences in exotic locations. These are probably fun, but you'll pay a lot less if you plan and book your vacations the normal way.

And you should avoid paying thousands of dollars for software trading programs and seminars.

Are all of these things scams?

Most of them don't qualify for that word. Their promoters may very well be sincere.

The Wall Street Journal, Money Magazine, Barron's, Kiplinger, and other such publications are certainly not scams.

But that doesn't make them any more accurate or necessary to build your retirement portfolio.

Learn to ignore such headlines as "The 10 Stocks You Need to Buy Now."

Stick with your plan. Put your extra money into your retirement account, where it belongs.

Financial Advisors are Another Unnecessary Expense

The financial advice industry is booming and will continue to boom until all the baby boomers are retired.

It's depressing how many people are going to pay a substantial chunk of their retirement—not all at once, but over the years—to hear financial advice they don't need.

I remember sitting in on a meeting with my mother and her broker at the time. He was telling her about a high tech stock she didn't need. "But Yahoo Finance says it's going to grow a lot," he had the nerve to say in front of me.

I hate to think how many thousands of dollars she paid to hear advice taken from Yahoo Finance!

That may sound unfair, but the truth is, financial advisors don't know the future either any more than do mutual fund managers and every other stock picking guru on TV, the Internet or the radio.

I will say if you need help organizing your finances, getting out of debt, setting up a budget, determining how much life insurance you need, and things like that, a qualified financial advisor can help you.

But make sure they are a "fee only" advisor. That way you pay them a fair price for the time they spend with you, but they don't get a percentage of your assets, as some advisors do.

Also, don't choose advisors that receive a commission for selling you stocks or insurance. They're salespeople, not advisors.

Actively Traded Mutual Funds are Borderline Scams in My Opinion

I know the managers at actively traded mutual funds will never go to jail, but they're also after too much of your hard-earned money.

The average large cap, actively traded mutual fund trails the S&P 500, yet charges you large management expense fees. They force you to pay capital gains taxes to the IRS.

Never put your money into any mutual fund except an index fund. Vanguard generally has the lowest expense ratios.

You do have to pay a small commission to buy stock. Your broker deserves some compensation for accessing the stock exchange on your behalf. But keep it low. (As I mentioned, I pay only $7 per trade.) And put in only "Buy" orders. Don't sell unless your back is up against the wall.

If you open a Vanguard S&P 500 Index fund account, Vanguard deserves a small management fee. Vanguard is one of the few mutual fund families that really works hard to keep its management fees as low as possible.

If you receive dividends outside of a tax-deferred account, you have to pay taxes to the federal government and, perhaps, your state government. (Ask your tax advisor about your state tax laws.)

That's it. You don't need to pay high expenses to an actively traded mutual fund, or high brokerage commissions, or for a subscription to The Wall Street Journal (unless it helps you in your business or on the job), or to pay a financial advisor for investment advice, or anything else.

You need to buy as many shares of the S&P 500 Index fund or dividend paying stocks as you can.

Another person who desperately wants your retirement money is Uncle Sam.

But if you never sell, you never have to pay capital gains taxes.

Chapter 28

The Tax Consequences of Stock Investing

It should come as no surprise the government (certainly the United States federal government, and about all other governments in the world) are keenly interested in anything that has to do with your money.

And that includes your investments.

First, a few basic definitions:

If you sell a stock for a profit, you have what's called a capital gain.

If you receive dividends, they are income.

1. Capital gains and income inside of a tax-deferred account or a Roth IRA are not taxable until you withdraw the money after age 59 1/2. That's the whole point of them.

2. If you have a capital gain from selling stock in a taxable brokerage account, and you held that stock less than one year, it's a short-term capital gain and it's taxed as your ordinary tax rate. (Same as wages and other such income.)

3. If you have a capital gain from selling stock in a taxable brokerage account, and you held that stock for longer than one year, it's a long-term

capital gain. The tax rate is 5% if you're in the lower two tax brackets. The tax rate is 15% if you're in the highest income bracket.

4. If you sell a stock for less than you paid for it, you have a capital loss. You can offset it against capital gains, so you pay taxes only on the net gain.

There's also some tricky things you can to with your past and future tax returns. See a tax professional.

5. Dividends from almost every US corporation qualify to be taxed at only 15%.

6. If you have a mutual fund you may be forced to pay capital gains taxes. The company will send you a check (or reinvest it into additional shares if you tell them to) late in the year.

In January the next year they'll send you a 1099 which says how many long term capital gains and how many short term capital gains you received in your account. You must pay taxes on these.

It does NOT mean you sold any of your mutual fund shares. It means the fund manager sold shares of stock for a profit.

Whether it's a short term or long term capital gain depends on how long the fund owned the stock, not on how long you have owned the fund.

Index funds minimize this situation because they don't buy or sell unless forced to by a change in the index.

I've been telling you not to waste your time analyzing individual stocks because there's no evidence even the fancy experts beat the market, and you're not a fancy expert.

Here's how you should spend any extra time you have to devote to making more money—spend it making more money!

Chapter 29

What Will Increase Your Retirement Portfolio Balance More than Anything Else

It's not picking "winning" stocks.

It's how much money you invest while you're still working.

That may sound obvious. Of course the person who invests $1,000 a month will have more at age 65 than the person who invests $100 a month.

Here's my point:

Lots of people spend lots of time trying to beat the market by analyzing stocks, economic figures, discussing these issues online, reading The Wall Street Journal and Money Magazine, and so on.

I believe you'd be better off using the money you spend on financial newsletters, newspapers and magazines to buy more stocks with.

I believe you'd be better off using the time you could spend analyzing annual reports, reading about investments, and so on to more profitable use if you devote that effort to raising your income.

Raise your income and you can pay off more debts and invest more money.

In the long run you'll have more money.

So whether you want to work a part time job, sell things on eBay, get a college degree or higher degree, get certified in your field, develop additional skills, learn how to increase your business profits, or something else, that's up to you.

Now, do you want to accelerate your wealth building by focusing on stocks that pay dividends, or rely on growth stocks to have capital gains?

Chapter 30

Investing for Capital Gains or Income?

As I've mentioned, it's almost universally assumed stock "investing" meaning buying a stock now to sell it for a profit later.

It's how I used to think. It's how market commentators think. It's how stockbrokers think. It's how fund managers think. It's what your neighbor thinks.

And it's probably what you think, without even being consciously aware of it.

However, there is an alternative.

Income investing.

As I covered in Chapter 13, some stocks pay out dividends.

I advocate you buy only stocks that pay dividends, then hold them forever—or until they stop paying dividends.

Then you don't need to depend on the stock market going up and handing you capital gains.

Whether the market price goes up or down—and it will do both many times—you don't care, because you're getting paid to own the stock.

When you invest for capital gains, your emotions fluctuate between fear and greed. You're always asking yourself whether you should sell a winner and bank your profit before it disappears, or whether you should sell a loser before it goes down further.

When you invest for income, your greed tells you to keep the stock so you'll get the dividend income. You're afraid of not receiving the dividend so, again, you don't sell.

Suddenly your emotions are working together to build your portfolio, instead of fighting together.

And if you never sell, you never pay a sales commission or capital gains taxes.

And if you never sell, you don't have to worry about running out of money.

Consider this famous chart by Dr. Jerome Siegel, from his book Stocks for the Long Run:

http://www.esrresearch.com/stockmarketinthelongrun.html

You can see from 1800-2002 stocks returned far more than gold, cash, bonds, or Treasury bills.

However, you need to keep something in mind—in this chart, Dr. Seigel assumes all dividends are reinvested.

If you don't receive dividends, you can't reinvest them, and so this chart does not apply to your retirement portfolio.

As I explained in Chapter 13, dividends are paid out of a company's cash, and when it pays dividends it cannot use the money to expand the company.

So in theory, when a company pays dividends, it is reducing its future growth. That's why most companies that pay dividends are old and well-established. Many dividend paying stocks manage to keep their companies operating (and growing), while paying generous and ever-growing dividends. Pepsi is a great example of this. So is Altria.

And—still in theory—by reducing its future growth through paying dividends, a company reduces the growth of the market price of its stock.

In a perfect world where all investors were rational rather than ruled by fear and greed, this would be reality.

In the real world, however, although a company's financial numbers are important, they determine only 10-20% of its stock price.

The other 80 to 90% is based on the overall market trend.

In other words, in a bear market (such as now), good stocks go down as well as bad stocks. In a bull market, bad stocks go up as well as good stocks.

The truth is, there is no precise, exact one to one correspondence between a company hanging on to cash and its stock price going up.

In fact, studies have shown stocks paying dividends tend to grow in price MORE than "growth" stocks that don't pay dividends - with one exception.

That is the height of a bull market. In 1999 the price of high tech growth stocks rose faster than the price of stodgy "old" dividend paying stocks.

But dividend paying stocks didn't crash in the Tech Wreck of early 2000. High flying high tech and dot com stocks DID. Dramatically.

However, to me the biggest argument is simply—without dividends— you cannot make money from a stock without selling it.

(You can borrow on it, but then you no longer control it, and you have to pay the interest expense. And if you don't repay the principle, you lose the stock, which is the same as selling it.)

And once you sell some stock, you can't benefit from its future price increases.

But if it pays dividends, you receive a cash "reward" every quarter for owning it. So why sell?

And the issue of selling stock is always a difficult one.

If you have a profit, you have a voice inside you telling you to sell and take your cash before a bear market wipes out the profit. Another voice tells you to hang in there, so you can make even more money in the future.

Which voice is right?

Nobody knows until it's too late.

People who had a profit when the Dow broke 14,000 in October 2007 but didn't sell, were kicking themselves in 2008 - and even harder in March 2009 when the Dow went below 7,000, losing over half its value.

Yet it has come back about 5,000 points since then.

Investing to collect dividends saves you from that dilemma.

If you decide to never sell, you just keep cashing (or—even better— reinvesting) those dividends. As time goes by they go up.

If you reinvest them, they compound so your portfolio has more and more shares even if you're not injecting new cash into it.

The standard financial advice to elderly people who have a stock portfolio is they can "afford" to sell 4% of their portfolio every year.

In almost all scenarios (combinations of bull and bear markets into the future), they won't run out of money before they probably die.

But that's not certain—all these calculations are based on the past (the stock market averages a 10% return in the long run), and those advisors don't know the future.

Besides, elderly people don't know whether they have a "long run" ahead of them or not.

So many elderly people refuse to sell their stock portfolios. And who can blame them?

But if they own shares of stock which don't pay dividends, what is the benefit to them if they never sell it? They have an asset which could be worth quite a lot on paper, but they can't spend any of that money unless they sell the stock. And then they don't have it any more.

That's the crux of my argument in favor of income investing. It's fine for a stock to go up in price, but that won't put money into your pocket unless you sell it.

It may keep going up in price, but you can't profit from that because you sold your shares.

It's up to you. I'm sure if you buy the S&P 500 now it will be worth a lot more in twenty plus years, especially if you do reinvest the dividends (some stocks, though not all, in the S&P 500 do pay dividends). I think you'll be worth even more in twenty plus years if you focus on a diversified portfolio of stocks that pay dividends, but it's up to you.

Chapter 31

Final Recommendations

1. The stock market is too volatile for short term investing. Use it to invest for long-term retirement or other long-term goals, at least 10 years away. Preferably 20 or more.

Therefore, stock market investing is limited to retirement and far away college accounts.

2. First use whatever tax-deferred accounts are available to you.

That includes one at work, and a personal IRA or Roth IRA, and a Keogh or SEP or SEP IRA if you're self-employed.

At the very least, take any and all matching funds you can qualify to receive from your employer. Not doing that is literally throwing money away.

3. Invest in indexes. This could include an index mutual fund or Exchange Traded Fund.

Work-related tax-deferred accounts will limit your choices. In your own brokerage account you can invest in Exchange Traded Funds.

4. If you have only a little money to start with, put it into a Dividend Re-Investment Plan.

5. Contribute the legal maximum to your tax-deferred accounts.

6. If you can afford to invest more money, use a regular brokerage account or contact a mutual fund.

7. Invest as much money as you can afford to.

8. Use your spare time to increase your income. Once it goes up, increase the amount you invest.

9. If I could not convince you income investing is the smartest way to go, put all your money into Vanguard's S&P 500 Index mutual fund or open a brokerage account and buy SPDR ETF shares.

Reinvest all dividends and any capital gains.

(The S&P 500 as a whole is not an income investment, but companies in it do pay dividends.)

10. If you do see the light and want to invest for income, open a brokerage account and buy Exchange Traded Funds for the best income investments such as Real Estate Investment Trusts, consumer stocks, utilities and so on.

(I'm not covering this in detail, because that is the point of my book Income Investing Secrets. This book is for stock market beginners, to get you started on the right foot.)

Reinvest all dividends.

Keep investing all you can (while staying out of debt) for the next ten, twenty, thirty, forty or more years. The longer you invest money and reinvest your profits, the bigger your portfolio will become. When you retire, live on only the income. Never sell the stocks sending you the dividends.

Chapter 32

Additional Investing Resources

Income Investing Secrets by Richard Stooker

This is my complete program for income investors.

A Random Walk Down Wall Street by Burton Malkiel

This is the book describing the Efficient Market Hypothesis.

Capital Ideas by Peter Bernstein

This is a complete history of modern finance theory.

Fooled by Randomness: The Hidden Role of Chance in Life and in the Markets by Nassim Nicholas Taleb

Philosophical, but reinforces the idea the market is (mostly) random and unpredictable.

A Mathematician Plays The Stock Market by John Allen Paulos

This is a fun but valuable look at how even those who know better can let their emotions take over.

Common Sense on Mutual Funds: Fully Updated 10th Anniversary

Edition by John C. Bogle and David F. Swensen

I barely skimmed the surface of how expensive actively managed mutual funds are. John Bogle founded Vanguard and is the pioneer of index funds, and here he is at his best exposing the flaws of the rest of the mutual fund industry. The only thing I disagree with him is how he dismisses Exchange Traded Funds.

I must also mention my main website and blog:

Income Investing Secrets

http://www.incomeinvesthome.com/

Income Investing Secrets blog

http://www.incomeinvestingsecrets.com/

The End

INCOME INVESTING SECRETS

While the financial markets are collapsing...

An Alton Illinois widow and grandmother of two is cashing ever-growing checks, enjoying a secure retirement and living the good life.

Just as she has through every bear market, stock crash and financial fad since 1955 — humiliating the Wall Street pros even though she couldn't analyze a company balance sheet if her life depended on it!

Finally, you too can discover her old-fashioned — yet now revolutionary (and updated for the 21st century) — "gold" egg income investing secrets for lazy investors

Despite following the conventional financial wisdom, many senior citizens are now asking what happened to that worry-free fun and relaxation they promised themselves after a long career of hard work.

Many people in their fifties and early sixties are wondering when — or even if — they'll be able to retire.

What's the alternative?

Investing for income.

Learn how to make money whether the stock market goes up, down or sideways.

"Rick Stooker is on the right track. We also intend to pursue a more income-oriented strategy in the years to come. Capital gains are subject to both the risk of a decline in economic fundamentals and a deterioration in market psychology. High-quality dividends and income are subject only to the former, and that makes a big difference in modeling your portfolio returns in retirement."

— *Charles Lewis Sizemore, CFA* **Senior Analyst, HS Dent Investment Management, LLC**

"I am a Chartered Accountant in Canada and spent most of my career teaching in a community college.

"Over the years, I have used various "plans," with varying degrees of success, but had never given much thought to dividends, so I fell prey to the hype about capital gains. So what was I thinking? Should have been investing for dividends.

"I also learned about some new investment vehicles, and got a "heads up" on some investments that I was aware of, but put on the back burner.

"Wish I knew about all this stuff when I was in my 20's, or at least paid attention to the theories involved in my 40's."

—- *Dennis Wilson*

"What an eye-opener!!!"

"I had heard about REITs, MLPs, BDCs, but you really explained their advantages and disadvantages. Thank you, Rick. You have set me on the right path to generate a steady income stream."

— *Kenny H*

Master Limited Partnerships

In a low yield world where government bonds pay next to no interest, S&P 500 stocks pay little more than that in dividends, the Canadian government is on the threshold of taxing income trusts, and even real estate investment trusts are suffering cash flow problems, one type of security still stands as a beacon of hope to income investors.

Master Limited Partnerships — MLPs

Until now, the information available to investors has been scanty. There've been only chapters in books. One prominent financial advice company recently launched a newsletter devoted to them, but the price tag is $399 annually. The Internet contains summary but incomplete articles and snatches of advice (some good, some inaccurate).

Finally, investors can learn all about these terrific investments — their rewards and risks; the paperwork hassles and how to get around them; and how to invest in them using both taxable and tax-deferred accounts —

In one convenient volume for one low price. This book is the first and only.

You'll discover:

The incredible benefits of Master Limited Partnerships

Why they're still incredibly cheap

How their legal rules and business structure combine to send you lots of cash

Why they'll continue to generate lots of cash for the foreseeable future

Information on every company

Information on every MLP index

Information on every MLP closed-end fund

What MLP i-units are and how they can skyrocket your IRA portfolio

How to understand and complete MLP tax forms

Everything you need to know to get started to enhance your current income or   save for your financially secure future.

Bring on the Crash!

A 3-Step Practical Survival Guide: Prepare for Economic Collapse and Come Out Wealthier

The U.S. dollar is on the verge of catastrophe.

For the first time in history, the debt of the most powerful government on Earth, leading the world's largest economy, has been downgraded by Standard & Poor's to Double AA from a perfect Triple AAA.

The political grandstanding of the Republicans and Democrats over the debt ceiling made many Americans and others around the world doubt our leadership. And many feel the final deal between doesn't go far enough to reduce US government spending.

US government debt now equals the Gross Domestic Product (GDP).

The 2007-2009 financial crisis appears to have been the first step toward a deflationary depression that could destroy the savings of three generations of Americans. We've technically been "recovering" since March 2009, but despite all government and Fed actions to stimulate the US economy, unemployment stubbornly remains over 9%.

China still owns many billions of US dollars of long-term Treasury bonds and is clearly worried about the future. They are making a big show of supporting Europe's economy, so they have an alternative to the US dollar. What is wrong with us when the biggest Communistic country on Earth has to lecture us on how to manage our currency?

How much longer will China, Japan and international bankers continue to buy U.S. Treasury bonds to finance our swelling budget?

If these countries began selling US dollars instead of buying, the hyperinflation would bankrupt America.

We – and Europeans – are also threatened by the debt problems of Europe. Greece nearly went up in flames over austerity measures forced on that country. Italy, Spain, Portugal and Ireland are also in bad shape. How long will France and German taxpayers continue to support them? If the euro breaks up, that will create more financial instability for the entire world.

Gold recently hit a record high of $1,813 per ounce.

Bring on the Crash! offers a 3 part process to protect yourself and your family from these dangers.

Whether you have $2,000 or $2 million, this volume contains all the resources you need to make sure you weather the coming storm.

This 3 step process is a comprehensive plan to survive almost all financial emergencies the US dollar is now facing.

www.ingramcontent.com/pod-product-compliance
Lightning Source LLC
Chambersburg PA
CBHW051543170526
45165CB00002B/853